AF501909

THE TEACHER'S BEST FRIEND

ELA SKILLS

HIGH SCHOOL COMMON CORE READING STANDARDS DECONSTRUCTED

- Daily Skill-Focused Objectives
- Aligned Measurable Tasks
- ACT Standard Connections

Chelsey Blue Spicer

Skippable Introduction

Year after year, I meet with teachers holding up pages of complex standards. We lean over the pages deconstructing the expectations into smaller pieces before we begin to plan their lesson. Every conversation ends in a similar way: if only there were something out there that had the pieces already identified, it would save us so much time.

The purpose of this book is to be a daily go-to resource for your instructional planning. All skills are deconstructed from the Common Core reading standards. It is important to check your state standards for possible subtle additions you may need to add to meet your state's requirements. However, the skills within this book create a solid foundation for daily instruction.

Within these pages, each standard is broken down into individual skills to meet all the requirements of the Common Core reading standards. The skills are organized in order of complexity for student mastery and should be referenced as a step-by-step guide to teaching individual standards across the four years of high school. While the skills are scaffolded per standard, it is crucial to understand that the order of the standards should not be taught numerically. Consult your school's curriculum guides before following these skills in order.

Accompanying each skill is a focused objective and an aligned measurable task for determining student understanding. The objectives state the specific skill students will be able to complete at the end of a daily lesson. Objectives begin with one of the Common Language Verbs found on the following pages. The verb demonstrates exactly what is expected of a student when a specific verb is used. Furthermore, the measurable tasks are activities to be completed at the end of the lesson to demonstrate knowledge for the skill. With many states using the ACT as a state assessment, each skill also possesses the aligned ACT standard at the 500 level. This book does not deconstruct ACT standards, however, I felt it was important to show where the correlation took place.

My greatest hope is this reference guide eases your load by streamlining aligned planning. This way you can spend time on the fun stuff, like what text to use and what cooperative learning strategy would best engage your unique class of young adults.

Where can you find the standard?

Common Language Verbs	7
RL.1	11
RL.2	17
RL.3	25
RL.4	31
RL.5	37
RL.6	43
RL.7	49
RL.9	53
RI.1	61
RI.2	67
RI.3	75
RI.4	83
RI.5	91
RI.6	97
RI.7	101
RI.8	105
RI.9	111

Common Language Verbs

Verbs are great, but knowing what you mean by them is crucial. The provided verbs are described to explain what a student is expected to do when used. All skills begin with a specific verb that links directly to this list of actions.

Identify
Student will select the best option from limited options.

Determine
Student will select the best option without pre-provided options.

Explain
Student will clarify exactly what is said to eliminate any obscurity in their own words.

Analyze
Student will separate something complex into its elements to explain them.

Evaluate
Student will assess the components of something complex for its value in relation to the total composition.

Develop
Student will improve or alter a scaffolded product.

Create
Student will put product into existence without any scaffolds.

Reading for Literature

Students should be able to locate evidence in a text that supports a claim about what the text says. They should be able to locate direct evidence from the text that completely supports the claim. Additionally, students need to be able to create inferences from the text to use as evidence for the claim. In higher level courses, students need to also be able to identify where the author left any matter(s) uncertain.

Identify explicit evidence from a small section of text to support a claim

ACT Connection	Objective
CLR 501	Students will be able to identify evidence that explicitly supports a claim.

Measurable Task

Provide students with prelabeled possible answers within a text excerpt from which to select.

Identify evidence from a small section of text to support an inference claim

ACT Connection	Objective
CLR 501	Students will be able to identify evidence that supports an inference claim.

Measurable Task

Provide students with prelabeled possible answers within a text excerpt from which to select.

Identify thorough evidence from a text to support a claim

ACT Connection	Objective
CLR 502	Students will be able to identify evidence that explicitly supports a claim.

Measurable Task

Provide multiple choice answer options with multiple answers that are correct. The correct answer contains all pieces of information, while the others address portions of the claim but not all parts.

Identify strong evidence from a text to support a claim

ACT Connection	Objective
CLR 502	Students will be able to identify the strongest evidence to support a claim.

Measurable Task

Provide students with a paragraph prelabeled possible answers. The correct answer will most clearly address the claim. It is critical to add the word "strongest" or "best".

Determine explicit evidence from a text to support a claim

ACT Connection	Objective
CLR 501	Students will be able to determine evidence in a text to explicitly support a claim.

Measurable Task

Provide students with a claim for them to support by underlining or highlighting evidence in a text without pre-identified possible answers.

Determine evidence from a text to support an inference claim

ACT Connection	Objective
CLR 505 & 506	Students will be able to determine evidence in a text to support an inference claim.

Measurable Task

Provide students with a claim for them to support by underlining or highlighting evidence in a text without pre-identified possible answers.

Determine thorough evidence from a text to support a claim

ACT Connection	Objective
CLR 505 & 506	Students will be able to determine evidence in a text that thoroughly supports a claim.

Measurable Task

Provide students with a claim for them to support by underlining or highlighting evidence in a text without pre-identified possible answers.

Determine strong evidence from a text to support a claim

ACT Connection	Objective
CLR 505 & 506	Students will be able to determine the strongest evidence in a text to support a claim.

Measurable Task

Provide students with a claim for them to support by underlining or highlighting evidence in a text without pre-identified possible answers.

Determine evidence that leaves a situation or the author's position uncertain

ACT Connection	Objective
CLR 501	Students will be able to determine evidence in a text that leaves the reader uncertain of the purpose.

Measurable Task

Provide students with a claim for them to support by underlining or highlighting evidence in a text without pre-identified possible answers.

Students will be able to determine the theme/central idea of a text without being given options. They will use details from the text to support the theme/central idea showing where the theme/central idea begins and how it is shaped by specific events over the course of a text. Using this information, a student should be able to create an objective summary of the text.

Identify a theme or central idea

ACT Connection	Objective
IDT 502	Students will be able to identify a theme or central idea of a text.

Measurable Task

Provide students with several thematic/central idea options, and have them select the option that is *best.*

Determine a theme or central idea

ACT Connection	Objective
IDT 501	Students will be able to determine a theme of a text. Students will be able to determine a central idea of a text.

Measurable Task

Students compose a statement identifying the theme or central idea of the text.

Identify the emergence of a theme

ACT Connection	Objective
CLR 502	Students will be able to identify the place in the text that first indicates its theme.

Measurable Task

Provide students with a paragraph containing prelabeled possible answers. The correct answer will address most clearly the claim. It is critical to add the word "strongest" or "best".

Identify the emergence of a central idea

ACT Connection	Objective
CLR 502	Students will be able to identify the place in the text that first indicates the central idea of a text.

Measurable Task

Provide students with a paragraph containing prelabeled possible answers. The correct answer will be the first instance that the central idea emerges.

Determine the emergence of a theme

ACT Connection	Objective
CLR 502	Students will be able to determine the place in the text that first indicates the theme of a text

Measurable Task

Students compose a statement identifying the emergence of theme.

Determine the emergence of a central idea

ACT Connection	Objective
CLR 502	Students will be able to determine the place in the text that first indicates the central idea of a text.

Measurable Task

Students compose a statement identifying the emergence of central idea.

Analyze how a theme or central idea emerges in a text

ACT Connection	Objective
TST 501	Students will be able to analyze how a theme/central idea emerges in a text.

Measurable Task

Students state the point of thematic emergence and compose a sentence or two about how this instance is the first time the reader would see the theme.

Analyze how a theme or central idea is shaped over the course of a text

ACT Connection	Objective
TST 503	Students will be able to analyze how a theme/central is shaped over the course of the text.

Measurable Task

Provide students with a graphic organizer. Students identify multiple points that the theme/central idea is being demonstrated in the text in section 1. Then, they compose a sentence or two about how each point aides in understanding the theme/central idea.

Analyze how specific details refine a theme or central idea

ACT Connection	Objective
TST 501	Students will be able to analyze how a specific detail refines a theme/central idea.

Measurable Task

Provide students with a graphic organizer. Students identify a point that the theme/central idea is being demonstrated in the text. Then they compose a sentence or two about how this point makes the theme/central idea very clear.

Identify multiple themes or central ideas in a single text

ACT Connection	Objective
IDT 502	Students will be able to identify more than one theme/central idea within a single text.

Measurable Task

Provide students with several thematic options and have them select all options that are themes/central ideas in the text.

Determine multiple themes or central ideas in a single text

ACT Connection	Objective
IDT 501	Students will be able to determine multiple themes/central ideas within a text.

Measurable Task

Students compose a statement identifying each of the possible themes/central ideas of the text.

Identify how multiple themes or central ideas in a single text interact with each other to create a complex account

ACT Connection	Objective
IDT 502	Students will be able to identify how multiple themes/central ideas create a complex account.

Measurable Task

Provide students with several explanations concerning how the multiple themes/central ideas specifically create complexity within the text provided, and have them select the best option.

Determine how multiple themes or central ideas in a single text interact with each other to create a complex account

ACT Connection	Objective
IDT 501	Students will be able to determine how multiple themes/ central ideas create a complex account.

Measurable Task

Students compose a statement about how the multiple themes/central ideas in a provided text, create a complex account through their interactions.

Identify how multiple themes or central ideas in a single text build on each other to create a complex account

ACT Connection	Objective
IDT 502	Students will be able to identify how a multiple themes/ central ideas build on each others to create a complex account.

Measurable Task

Provide students with several explanations concerning how the multiple themes/central ideas specifically create complexity within the text provided, and have them select the best option.

Determine how multiple themes or central ideas in a single text build on each other to create a complex account

ACT Connection	Objective
IDT 501	Students will be able to determine how multiple themes/ central ideas create a complex account.

Measurable Task

Students compose a statement about how the multiple themes/central ideas in a provided text create a complex account by building on each other.

Develop an objective summary

ACT Connection	Objective
IDT 503	Students will develop an objective summary

Measurable Task

Provide students a guide or graphic organizer to outline the components of an objective summary to complete.

Create an objective summary

ACT Connection	Objective
IDT 503	Students will create an objective summary

Measurable Task

Students compose an objective summary identifing the theme/central idea and outline key details.

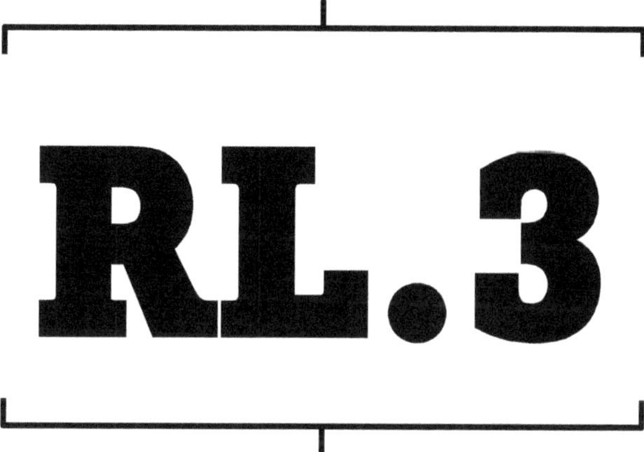

Students will be able identify a complex character and explain how throughout the text the character changed, interacted with other characters, and influenced the plot of the story. In higher level courses, students will analyze the impact an author's choice to introduce characters has on the text.

Identify a complex character

ACT Connection	Objective
CLR 504	Students will be able to identify a complex character.

Measurable Task

Provide students with multiple characters to identify which is the complex character.

Determine a complex character within a text

ACT Connection	Objective
CLR 504	Students will be able to determine a complex character within a text.

Measurable Task

Provide students with a claim about a complex character. Students must support the claim by underlining or highlighting evidence in a text without pre-identified possible answers.

Analyze a complex character's motivations

ACT Connection	Objective
REL 504	Students will be able to analyze a complex character's motivations

Measurable Task

Provide students with a graphic organizer to complete an analysis by explaining specific moments of motivation. Then have students create a connecting statement linking the motivations into the bigger picture of the story.

Analyze a complex character's interaction with other characters

ACT Connection	Objective
REL 503	Students will be able to analyze a complex character's interaction with other characters.

Measurable Task

Provide students with a graphic organizer that has students analyze the interactions between the complex character and another character. Then have students create a connecting statement linking the motivations to the bigger picture of the story.

Analyze how a complex character advances a plot

ACT Connection	Objective
REL 504	Students will be able to analyze how a complex character advances a plot.

Measurable Task

Provide students with a graphic organizer to complete by explaining a complex character's impact on specific plot points. Then have students create a connecting statement linking the character to the advancement of the plot.

Skills continue on the following page.

Analyze how a complex character develops a theme

ACT Connection	Objective
REL 504	Students will analyze how a complete character develops a theme.

Measurable Task

Provide students with a graphic organizer that has students analyze the complex character's impact on specific plot points. Then have students create a connecting statement that links the character to the advancement of the theme.

Analyze the impact of an author's choice of how the story is set develops the text

ACT Connection	Objective
REL 502	Students will be able to analyze the author's choice to set a story in a certain location develops the story.

Measurable Task

Provide students with a graphic organizer that has students analyze the author's impact of the setting on specific events. Then have students create a connecting statement linking the setting to the development of the text.

Students will be able to determine the meaning of a word or phrase by using context clues in the text. This includes figurative language and words with multiple meanings. In higher level courses, students will also be able to analyze the impact certain words have on the story's theme and its tone.

Identify the meaning of words as used in the text

ACT Connection	Objective
WME 503	Students will be able to identify the meaning of a word using context clues.

Measurable Task

Have students identify the best definition from several options.

Determine the meaning of words as used in the text

ACT Connection	Objective
WME 503	Students will be able to determine the meaning of a word using context clues.

Measurable Task

Have students state or compose a statement defining the word as it is used in the text.

Identify the connotative meaning of words as used in the text

ACT Connection	Objective
WME 503	Students will be able to identify the connotative meaning of a word using context clues.

Measurable Task

Have students identify the definition of the word as it is used in context, not the literal definition.

Determine the connotative meaning of words as used in the text

ACT Connection	Objective
WME 503 & 504	Students will be able to determine the connotative meaning of a word in context.

Measurable Task

Have students state or compose a statement determining the meaning of a word as it is being used in the text that matches the purpose and tone.

Analyze the multiple meanings of a word as used in a text

ACT Connection	Objective
WME 501	Students will analyze the multiple meanings of a word as used in a text.

Measurable Task

Provide students a graphic organizer to define the multiple meanings of a particular word in the text in one space. Then have students explain each meaning's impact on the passage.

Identify the meaning of phrases as used in the text

ACT Connection	Objective
WME 503	Students will be able to identify the meaning of a phrase using context clues.

Measurable Task

Have students select the best meaning of the phrase from several options.

Determine the meaning of phrases as used in the text

ACT Connection	Objective
WME 503	Students will be able to determine the meaning of a phrase in context.

Measurable Task

Have students state or compose a statement determining the meaning of a phrase as it is being used in the text that matches the purpose and tone.

Identify the meaning of figurative language as used in the text

ACT Connection	Objective
WME 503	Students will be able to identify the meaning of figurative language using context clues.

Measurable Task

Have students select the best definition from several options.

Determine the meaning of figurative language as used in the text

ACT Connection	Objective
WME 504	Students will be able to determine the meaning of figurative language in context.

Measurable Task

Students compose a statement determining the meaning of figurative language as it is being used in the text that matches the purpose and tone.

Analyze the multiple meanings of phrases as used in a text

ACT Connection	Objective
WME 501	Students will analyze the multiple meanings of a phrase as used in a text.

Measurable Task

Provide students a graphic organizer to define the multiple meanings of a particular phrase in the text in one space. Then students must explain each meaning's impact on the passage.

Analyze the cumulative impact of specific word choices on meaning

ACT Connection	Objective
WME 501	Students will analyze a specific phrase or words cumulative impact on the meaning of the text.

Measurable Task

Provide students with a graphic organizer in which the students define the phrase or word, describe the tone of the word in use, and explain how the word impacts the meaning of the text.

Analyze the cumulative impact of specific word choices on tone

ACT Connection	Objective
WME 51	Students will analyze the cumulative impact a specific word or text has on the tone of the text.

Measurable Task

Provide students with a graphic organizer in which the students define the phrase or word, describe the tone of the word in use, and explain how the word impacts the tone of the whole text.

Students should be able to analyze the organization and structure of a text and determine the impacts they make on meaning. In higher level courses, students should be able to recognize when a timeline is manipulated and discuss why an author chose to begin in a specific place instead of another. They should also determine why the author ended the story the way they did.

Identify order of events within a text

ACT Connection

REL 501

Objective

Students will be able to identify the order of events within a text.

Measurable Task

From a list of options, students should select the option with the correct sequence of events or be able to identify which event would follow one identified.

Determine order of events within a text

ACT Connection

REL 501

Objective

Students will be able to determine the order of events within a text.

Measurable Task

Provide students with a text excerpt. Then have the students sort events into chronological order.

Identify elements of foreshadowing within a text

ACT Connection

PPV 501

Objective

Students will be able to identify elements of foreshadowing within a text.

Measurable Task

From a list of options, students select the element of foreshadowing for a provided outcome.

Determine the structures of a text

ACT Connection	Objective
TST 503	Students will be able to determine specific text structures.

Measurable Task

Students are able to locate significant structures within a provided text, such as a flashback or time shift, etc.

Analyze how an author's choices of text structure create effects of mystery

ACT Connection	Objective
TST 502	Students will be able to analyze how an author's choice of text structure creates an effect of mystery.

Measurable Task

Provide students a graphic organizer to identify three structures the author uses to build mystery. For each structure, have the students state the effect of the structure then explain how that structure builds a sense of mystery.

Analyze how an author's choices of text structure creates tension

ACT Connection	Objective
PPV 501	Students will be able to analyze how an author's choice of text structure creates tension.

Measurable Task

Provide students a graphic organizer to identify three structures the author uses to build tension. For each structure, have the students state the effect of the structure and have them explain how that structure builds a sense of tension.

Analyze why an author chooses to structure specific parts of a text to build its overall structure

ACT Connection	Objective
TST 502	Students will be able to analyze why an author chooses to structure a specific part of a text to built its overall structure.

Measurable Task

Provide students a text excerpt. Students should identify any specific text structures used in the excerpt, explain in their own words what the structures are doing. Then students must explain how the structure impacts the text as a whole. This task is Ideal for long passage, short story with several text structures or a novel.

Analyze why an author chooses to structure specific parts of a text contribute to the overall aesthetic

ACT Connection	Objective
TST 502	Students will be able to analyze why an author chooses to structure a specific part of a text contributes to the overall aesthetic.

Measurable Task

Provide students a text excerpt. Students should identify any specific text structures used in the excerpt, explain in their own words what the structures are doing. Then students should explain how the structure impacts the aesthetic. This task is Ideal for long passage, short story several text structures or a novel.

RL.6

Students should be able to analyze how point of view and cultural experiences are presented in literature from outside the United States and across multiple cultures. In higher level courses, students need to be able to identify elements of irony, sarcasm, and understatement. Students should also able to determine the connotative meaning in satirical texts.

Analyze point of view from a work outside of United States literature

ACT Connection	Objective
PPV 501	Students will be able to analyze a point of view from a work outside of United States literature.

Measurable Task

Provide students a graphic organizer to compare the point of view of the text to the presentation of a point of view in US literature.

Analyze cultural experience reflecting a work of literature from outside of United States literature

ACT Connection	Objective
PPV 501	Students will be able to analyze a cultural experience from a literary work outside of United States literature.

Measurable Task

Provide students a graphic organizer to compare the cultural understanding of the text to the presentation of culture in US literature.

Identify a work of satire

ACT Connection	Objective
PPV 502	Students will be able to identify a work of satire.

Measurable Task

From a list of options, students should select the option that identifies the work as satire.

Determine if a work is satire

ACT Connection	Objective
PPV 502	Students will be able to determine if a work is satire.

Measurable Task

Student states or composes a statement that states a text is a work of satire.

Identify sarcasm within a text

ACT Connection	Objective
PPV 502	Students will be able to identify sarcasm within a text.

Measurable Task

From a list of options, students should select the option that is a sarcastic statement.

Determine elements of irony within a text

ACT Connection	Objective
PPV 502	Students will be able to determine elements of irony within a text.

Measurable Task

Provide students with an excerpt of a text and have students underline or highlight evidence without pre-identified possible answers that demonstrate irony.

Determine elements of understatement within a text

ACT Connection	Objective
PPV 502	Students will be able to determine elements of understatement within a text.

Measurable Task

Provide students with an excerpt of a text and have students underline or highlight evidence without pre-identified possible answers that demonstrate understatement.

Analyze a text's meaning in a satirical piece

ACT Connection	Objective
ARG 501	Students will be able to analyze a text's meaning in a satirical piece.

Measurable Task

Students develop a paragraph where they state the meaning of a satirical work, explains multiple pieces of evidence in the work, and explains how they contribute to the meaning of the text.

Analyze the meaning of irony within a text

ACT Connection	Objective
ARG 501	Students will be able to analyze the meaning of irony within a text.

Measurable Task

Students develop a paragraph where they state the meaning of a irony work, explain multiple pieces of evidence in the work, and explain how they contribute to the meaning of the text.

Analyze the meaning of sarcasm within a text

ACT Connection	Objective
ARG 501	Students will be able to analyze the meaning of sarcasm within a text.

Measurable Task

Students develop a paragraph where they state the meaning of sarcasm within a work, explain multiple pieces of evidence in the work, and explain how they contribute to the meaning of the text.

Analyze the impact of understatement within a text

ACT Connection	Objective
ARG 501	Students will be able to analyze the meaning of understatement within a text.

Measurable Task

Students develop a paragraph where they state the meaning of understatement within a work, explain multiple pieces of evidence in the work, and explain how they contribute to the meaning of the text.

RL.7

Students will be able to analyze scenes in two mediums of the same text. In higher level courses, students will be able to evaluate interpretations of an original text.

Determine differences between two artistic mediums on the same topic

ACT Connection	Objective
REL 503	Students will be able to determine the differences between two artistic mediums on the same topic.

Measurable Task

Provide students excerpts from two texts and have students will highlight or underline specific differences between the two texts.

Determine focus of emphasis within two artistic mediums on the same topic

ACT Connection	Objective
REL 503	Students will determine the focus of emphasis within two artistic mediums on the same topic.

Measurable Task

Provide students excerpts from two texts and have students will create a statement that identifies a common focus of emphasis within the two texts.

Analyze two artistic mediums on the same topic

ACT Connection	Objective
PPV 501	Students will analyze two artistic medium on the same topic.

Measurable Task

Students develop a paragraph where they state the common focus of medium, explain the commonalities, and explain the differences.

Analyze two interpretations of a text

ACT Connection	Objective
TST 505	Students will be able to analyze two interpretations of a text.

Measurable Task

Students develop a paragraph where they state the common focus of mediums, explain the commonalities, and explain the differences.

Evaluate the interpretation of a text

ACT Connection	Objective
TST 505	Students will be able to evaluate the interpretation of a text.

Measurable Task

Students analyze the commonalities and differences between the text, and explain the effectiveness of the interpretation on promoting the central idea of the original text in a paragraph.

Students will be able to analyze how an author uses another text within their work to create their story. In higher level courses, students will also be able to analyze ways in which various American literary texts treat similar topics.

Identify the use of a theme or topic from another text within a work

ACT Connection	Objective
PPV 502	Students will be able to identify the theme from another text.

Measurable Task

From a list of options, students should select the option that matches the common theme.

Determine the transformation of source material within a specific work

ACT Connection	Objective
PPV 501	Students will be able to determine the transformation of source material from a specific work.

Measurable Task

Providedstudents excerpts from two texts, and have students should highlight or underline the use of a secondary text.

Analyze how an author uses source material in a specific work

ACT Connection	Objective
TST 505	Students will be able to analyze how an author uses source material within a specific work.

Measurable Task

Students develop a paragraph where they identify the text referenced and explain how that text contributes to the work as a whole.

Analyze how an author transforms source material in a specific work

ACT Connection	Objective
TST 505	Students will be able to analyze how an author transforms source material in a specific work.

Measurable Task

Students develop a paragraph where they identify the text referenced and explain how that referenced text is transformed within the specific work.

Determine two texts from a similar time discuss a similar topic

ACT Connection	Objective
IDT 501	Students will be able to determine two texts from a similar time that discuss a similar topic.

Measurable Task

Students create a claim statement naming two texts that focus on a similar topic.

Analyze how two texts within a similar time discuss a similar topic

ACT Connection	Objective
TST 505	Students will be able to analyze how two texts within a similar time discuss a similar topic.

Measurable Task

Students create a paragraph where they identify two texts that discuss a similar topic and how each text focuses on the topic.

Analyze how two texts within a similar time discuss a similar theme

ACT Connection	Objective
TST 505	Students will be able to analyze how two texts within a similar time discuss a similar theme.

Measurable Task

Students complete a graphic organizer identifying two texts that discuss a similar theme and explaining how each text develops that theme.

Reading for Information

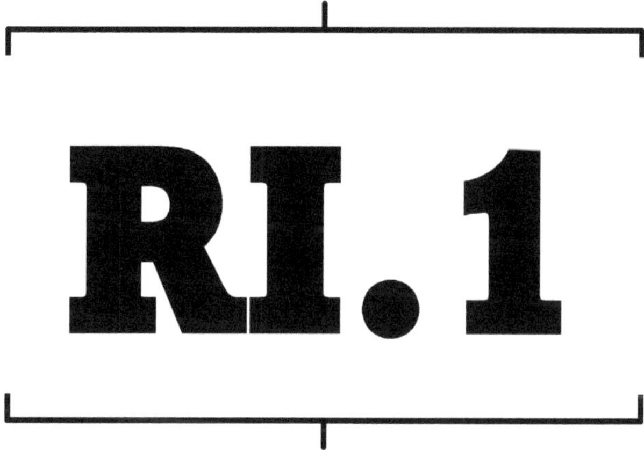

Students should be able to locate evidence in a text that supports a claim about what the text says. They should be able to locate direct evidence from the text that completely supports the claim. Additionally, students need to be able to create inferences from the text to use as evidence for the claim. In higher level courses, students need to be able to identify where the author left any matter(s) uncertain.

Identify explicit evidence from a small section of text to support a claim

ACT Connection	Objective
CLR 501	Students will be able to identify evidence that explicitly supports a claim.

Measurable Task

Provide students with prelabeled possible answers within a text excerpt from which to select.

Identify evidence from a small section of text to support an inference claim

ACT Connection	Objective
CLR 502	Students will be able to identify evidence that supports an inference claim.

Measurable Task

Provide students with prelabeled possible answers within a text excerpt from which to select.

Identify thorough evidence from a small section of text to support a claim

ACT Connection	Objective
CLR 502	Students will be able to identify evidence that thoroughly supports a claim.

Measurable Task

Provide multiple choice answer options with multiple correct answers. The correct answer contains all pieces of information, while the others address portions of the claim but not all parts.

Identify strong evidence from a small section of text to support a claim

ACT Connection	Objective
CLR 502	Students will be able to identify the strongest evidence to support a claim.

Measurable Task

Provide multiple choice answer options with multiple correct answers. The correct answer will most clearly address the claim. It is critical to add the word "strongest" or "best" to the questions to indicate to students that there is more than one possible correct answer, and they need to locate the most clear option.

Determine explicit evidence from a text to support a claim

ACT Connection	Objective
CLR 502	Students will be able to locate evidence in a text to explicitly support a claim.

Measurable Task

Provide students with a claim they must support by underlining or highlighting evidence in a text without pre-identified possible answers.

Determine evidence from a text to support an inference claim

ACT Connection	Objective
CLR 502	Students will be able to locate evidence in a text to support an inference claim.

Measurable Task

Provide students with a claim they must support by underlining or highlighting evidence in a text without pre-identified possible answers.

Determine thorough evidence from a text to support a claim

ACT Connection	Objective
CLR 502	Students will be able to locate evidence in a text that thoroughly supports a claim.

Measurable Task

Provide students with a claim they must support by underlining or highlighting evidence in a text without pre-identified possible answers.

Determine strong evidence from a text to support a claim

ACT Connection	Objective
CLR 502	Students will be able to locate the strongest evidence in a text to support a claim.

Measurable Task

Provide students with a claim they must support by underlining or highlighting evidence in a text without pre-identified possible answers.

Determine evidence that leaves a situation or the author's position uncertain

ACT Connection	Objective
CLR 503	Students will be able to locate evidence in a text that leaves the reader uncertain of the purpose.

Measurable Task

Provide students with a claim they must support by underlining or highlighting evidence in a text without pre-identified possible answers.

RI.2

Students will be able to determine the central idea of a text without being given options. They will use details from the text to support the central idea that show where the central idea begins and how it is shaped by specific events over the course of a text. Using this information, a student should be able to create an objective summary of the text.

Identify a central idea

ACT Connection	Objective
IDT 502	Students will be able to identify a central idea of a text.

Measurable Task
Provide students with several central idea options, and have them select the option that is *best.*

Determine a central idea

ACT Connection	Objective
IDT 501	Students will be able to determine a central idea of a text.

Measurable Task
Have students state the central idea of the text read in class.

Identify the emergence of a central idea

ACT Connection	Objective
IDT 501	Students will be able to identify the place in the text that first indicates the central idea of a text.

Measurable Task
Provide students with a paragraph that containing prelabeled possible answers. The correct answer will most clearly address the claim. It is critical to add the word "strongest" or "best".

Determine the emergence of a central idea

ACT Connection	Objective
IDT 501	Students will be able to determine the place in the text that first indicates the it's theme

Measurable Task

Have students compose a statement identifying the emergence of central idea in a written statement.

Analyze how a central idea emerges in a text

ACT Connection	Objective
ARG 501	Students will be able to analyze how a central idea emerges in a text.

Measurable Task

Students state the point from which the central idea emergences and compose a sentence or two about how this instance is the first time the reader would see the central idea.

Analyze how a central idea is shaped over the course of a text

ACT Connection	Objective
ARG 502	Students will be able to analyze how a central idea is shaped over the course of a text

Measurable Task

Students identify multiple points in the text in which the central idea is being demonstrated. Then they must compose a sentence about how each point aides in understanding the central idea.

Analyze how specific details refine a central idea

ACT Connection	Objective
ARG 501	Students will be able to analyze how specific details refine a central idea.

Measurable Task

Have students identify a point that in the text in which the central idea is being demonstrated. Then they compose a sentence or two about how this point makes the central idea very clear.

Identify multiple central ideas in a single text

ACT Connection	Objective
IDT 502	Students will be able to identify multiple central ideas in a single text.

Measurable Task

Provide students with several central idea options and have them select all options that are central ideas in the text.

Determine multiple central ideas in a single text

ACT Connection	Objective
IDT 501	Students will be able to determine multiple central ideas in a single text.

Measurable Task

Have students state each of the possible central ideas of the text read in class.

Identify how multiple central ideas in a single text interact with each other to create a complex account

ACT Connection	Objective
IDT 501	Students will be able to identify how multiple central ideas in a single text interact with each other to create a complex account.

Measurable Task

Provide students with several explanations concerning how multiple central ideas specifically create complexity within the text provided. Students will then select the best option.

Determine how multiple central ideas in a single text interact with each other to create a complex account

ACT Connection	Objective
REL 503	Students will be able to determine how multiple central ideas in a single text interact with each other to create a complex account.

Measurable Task

Have students compose a statement about how the interactions of multiple central ideas found within a text create a complex account.

Skills continue on the following page.

Identify how multiple central ideas in a single text build on each other to create a complex account

ACT Connection	Objective
REL 504	Students will be able to identify how multiple central ideas in a single text build on each other to create a complex account.

Measurable Task

Provide students with several explanations how multiple central ideas specifically create complexity within the text provided. Then have them select the best option.

Determine how multiple central ideas in a single text build on each other to create a complex account

ACT Connection	Objective
REL 503	Students will be able to determine how multiple central ideas in a single text build on each other to create a complex account.

Measurable Task

Students compose a statement identifying how the multiple central ideas in a provided text create a complex account by building on each other.

Develop an objective summary

ACT Connection	Objective
IDT 503	Students will be able to develop an objective summary.

Measurable Task

Provide students a guide or graphic organizer to aide the composition of an objective summary.

Create an objective summary

ACT Connection	Objective
IDT 503	Students will be able to create an objective summary

Measurable Task

Students compose an objective summary that identifies the central idea and outlines key details.

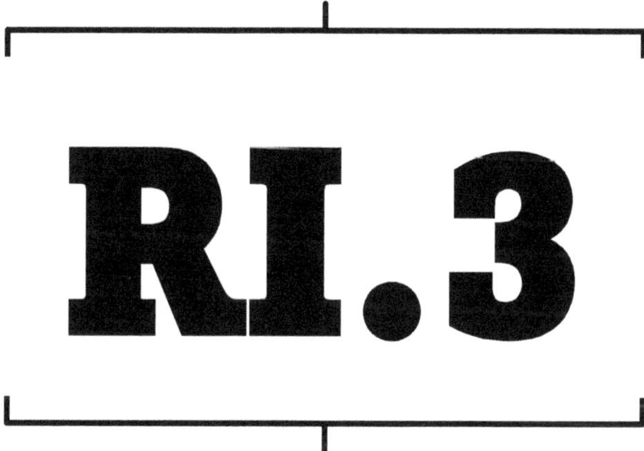

Students will be able to analyze the introduction, order and development of main ideas. Students will analyze the connections between main ideas. In the higher levels, students will be able to explain the inclusion of specific individuals, ideas, and events in a text.

Determine the order of main ideas made within a text

ACT Connection	Objective
REL 501	Students will be able to determine the order of main ideas made within a text.

Measurable Task

Have students create a statement that place main ideas in chronological order.

Analyze how the order of main ideas is presented within a text

ACT Connection	Objective
WME 401	Students will be able to analyze how the order of main ideas is presented within a text.

Measurable Task

Have students develop a paragraph that explain the importance of how main ideas are presented within a text.

Analyze how the main ideas are developed over the course of the text

ACT Connection	Objective
WME 402	Students will be able to analyze how the main ideas are developed over the course of a text.

Measurable Task

Have students develop a paragraph that explains how three main ideas are introduced and explains the purpose they serve in the text.

Determine the connections drawn between the main ideas of a text

ACT Connection	Objective
REL 502	Students will be able to determine the connections drawn between the main ideas of a text.

Measurable Task

Provide students with a graphic organizer to determine main ideas. Then students must create a connection statement between each of the main ideas.

Analyze the connections between the main ideas of a text

ACT Connection	Objective
REL 503	Students will be able to analyze the connections between the main ideas of a text.

Measurable Task

Have students determine two main ideas of a text, develop a connection statement, and explain the importance of the connection.

Identify a complex sequence of events

ACT Connection	Objective
REL 501	Students will be able to identify complex sequence of events.

Measurable Task

Provide students with a text with pre-identified events that are not presented in chronological order. Then have students put the events in chronological order.

Determine a complex sequence of events

ACT Connection	Objective
REL 501	Students will be able to determine a complex sequence of events.

Measurable Task

Provide students a text with complex event organization and ask them to organize the events chronologically.

Analyze how complex sequence of events interact over the course of the text

ACT Connection	Objective
TST 501	Students will be able to analyze how complex sequence of events interact over the course of the text.

Measurable Task

Provide students with a graphic organizer. Then students must determine three main events of a text, develop an interaction statement, and explain the importance of the interaction.

Analyze how a complex sequence of events develops over the course of the text

ACT Connection	Objective
TST 501	Students analyze how a complex sequences of events develops over the course of the text.

Measurable Task

Have students develop a paragraph that identify main events from a text, organize them chronologically, and explain the importance of the development between the ideas.

Analyze how a complex set of main ideas interact over the course of the text

ACT Connection	Objective
ARG 501	Students will be able to analyze how a complex set of main ideas interact over the course of the text.

Measurable Task

Have students determine three main ideas of a text, develop an interaction statement, and explain the importance of the interaction.

Analyze how a complex set of main ideas develops over the course of the text

ACT Connection	Objective
ARG 501	Students will be able analyze how a complex set of main ideas develops over the course of a text.

Measurable Task

Have students develop a paragraph that identify main ideas from a text, organize them chronologically, and explain the importance of the development between the ideas.

Analyze how specific individuals and/or events interact over the course of the text

ACT Connection	Objective
TST 502	Students will be able to analyze how specific individuals/events interact over the course of the text.

Measurable Task

Have students determine specific individuals/events in a text, develop an interaction statement, and explain the importance of the interaction.

Analyze how specific individuals and/or events develop over the course of the text

ACT Connection	Objective
TST 502	Students will be able to analyze how specific individuals/events develop over the course of a text.

Measurable Task

Have students develop a paragraph that identify specific individuals/events in a text, organize them chronologically, and explain the importance of the development between the ideas.

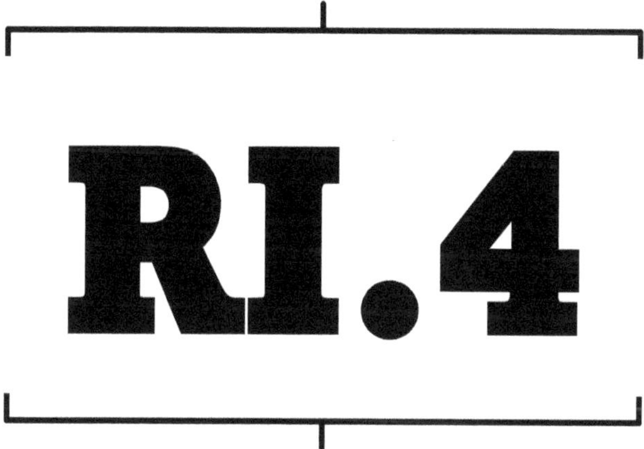

Students will be able to figure out the meaning of a word or phrase by using context clues in the text. This includes figurative language and words with multiple meanings. Students will be able to determine meaning of technical terms used in context. In higher level courses, students will be able to analyze the impact certain words have on the text's central idea and it's tone.

Identify the meaning of words as used in the text

ACT Connection	Objective
WME 503	Students will be able to identify the meaning of a word using context clues.

Measurable Task

Have students select the best definition from several options provided.

Determine the meaning of words as used in the text

ACT Connection	Objective
WME 503	Students will be able to determine the meaning of a word using context clues.

Measurable Task

Have students composes a statement that defines the word as it is used in the text.

Identify the connotative meaning of words as used in the text

ACT Connection	Objective
WME 504	Students will be able to identify the connotative meaning of a word using context clues.

Measurable Task

Have students select the definition of the word as it is used in context, not the literal definition.

Determine the connotative meaning of words as used in the text

ACT Connection	Objective
WME 504	Students will be able to determine the connotative meaning of a word in context.

Measurable Task

Student composes a statement that defines the meaning of a word as it is being used in the text, matching the purpose and tone.

Determine the technical meaning of words as used in the text

ACT Connection	Objective
WME 504	Students will be able to determine the technical meaning of a word in context.

Measurable Task

Student composes a statement concerning the meaning of a technical word as it is being used in the text, matching the purpose and tone.

Analyze the multiple meanings of a word as used in a text

ACT Connection	Objective
WME 502	Students will analyze the multiple meanings of a word as used in a text.

Measurable Task

Provide students a graphic organizer that has them define in one space the multiple meanings of a particular word in the text.

Identify the meaning of phrases as used in the text

ACT Connection	Objective
WME 503	Students will be able to identify the meaning of a phrase using context clues.

Measurable Task

Have students select the best meaning of the phrase from several options.

Determine the meaning of phrases as used in the text

ACT Connection	Objective
WME 504	Students will be able to determine the meaning of a phrase in context.

Measurable Task

Students compose a statement concerning the meaning of a phrase as it is being used in the text, matching the purpose and tone.

Identify the meaning of figurative language as used in the text

ACT Connection	Objective
WME 504	Students will be able to identify the meaning of figurative language using context clues.

Measurable Task

Have students select the best meaning of figurative language from several options.

Determine the meaning of figurative language as used in the text

ACT Connection	Objective
WME 504	Students will be able to determine the meaning of figurative language in context.

Measurable Task

Students compose a statement concerning the meaning of figurative language as it is being used in the text, matching the purpose and tone.

Analyze the multiple meanings of phrases as used in a text

ACT Connection	Objective
WME 502	Students will analyze the multiple meanings of a phrase as used in a text.

Measurable Task

Provide students a graphic organizer in which the students define the multiple meanings of a particular phrase in the text in one space, then explain each meaning's impact on the passage.

Analyze the cumulative impact of specific word choices on meaning

ACT Connection	Objective
WME 502	Students will analyze a specific phrase or words cumulative impact the meaning of the text.

Measurable Task

Provide students with a graphic organizer where in the student will define the word, describe the tone of the word in use, and explain how the word impacts the meaning of the text.

Analyze the cumulative impact of specific word choices on tone

ACT Connection	Objective
WME 502	Students will analyze a specific phrase or words cumulative impact the tone of the text.

Measurable Task

Provide students with a graphic organizer. Then students will define the phrase or word, describe the tone of the word in use, and explain how the word impacts the tone of the whole text.

RI.5

Students will be able to explain how the main ideas within a text developed by focusing on smaller sections within the text. In the higher levels, students will be able to evaluate how effective a text is and if the structure aides in clarity of points.

Determine how specific sentences develop author's ideas/claims

ACT Connection	Objective
TST 502	Students will be able to determine how specific sentences develop author's ideas/claims.

Measurable Task

Students compose a statement that explain the importance of a specific sentence in relation to the idea of the text.

Determine how paragraphs develop author's ideas/claims

ACT Connection	Objective
TST 503	Students will be able to determine how paragraphs develop author's ideas/claims.

Measurable Task

Students compose a statement that explain the importance of a specific paragraph in relation to the idea of the text.

Analyze how sections/or larger portions develop the author's claims within the text

ACT Connection	Objective
TST 505	Students will be able to analyze how sections/or larger portions develop the author's claims within the text.

Measurable Task

Students composes a statement that explain the importance of a specific section of text in relation to the idea of the text.

Analyze how paragraphs develop author's ideas/claims

ACT Connection	Objective
ARG 501	Students will be able to analyze how paragraphs develop author's ideas/claims.

Measurable Task

Students develop a paragraph that identifies specific paragraphs within the text, organizes them chronologically, and explains the importance of the development between the ideas.

Analyze structural elements of a text

ACT Connection	Objective
TST 505	Students will be able to analyze structural elements of a text.

Measurable Task

Students develop a paragraph that identifies structural elements in a text and explains the purpose they hold in the text.

Evaluate the structural elements of a text

ACT Connection	Objective
TST 505	Students will be able to evaluate the structural elements of a text.

Measurable Task

Students develop a paragraph that identifies structural elements of the text and explains the effectiveness of the development between ideas.

Analyze text features

ACT Connection	Objective
TST 501	Students will be able to analyze text features.

Measurable Task

Students develop a paragraph that identify the features of a text and explains their purpose.

Evaluate the effectiveness of text features

ACT Connection	Objective
TST 502	Students will be able to evaluate the effectiveness of text features.

Measurable Task

Students develop a paragraph that identify text features and explain the effectiveness of the development between the ideas.

RI.6

Students will be able determine the author's point of view and their use of rhetoric to advance the point of view. Students will also be able to determine the author's purpose and analyze the rhetoric used to advance the plot. In higher level courses, students will be able to analyze the effectiveness of the rhetoric in the creating a powerful, persuasive, or beautiful text.

Identify author's point of view

ACT Connection	Objective
PPV 501	Students will be able to identify author's point of view.

Measurable Task

Have students select the correct option from provided options.

Determine author's point of view in text

ACT Connection	Objective
PPV 502	Students will be able to determine author's point of view in text.

Measurable Task

Students compose a statement that correctly identifies the author's point of view.

Determine the use of rhetorical devices within a text.

ACT Connection	Objective
PPV 501	Students will be able to determine the use of rhetorical devices within a text.

Measurable Task

Have students compose a statement that identifies rhetorical devices within a text.

Determine how an author uses rhetorical devices to advance point of view

ACT Connection	Objective
TST 505	Students will be able to determine how an author uses rhetoric to advance point of view.

Measurable Task

Students compose a statement identifying a rhetorical device and explain how the author uses rhetoric to advance the point of view.

Analyze how style contributes to effectiveness of text

ACT Connection	Objective
TST 505	Students will be able to analyze how style contributes to effectiveness of text.

Measurable Task

Students compose a statement that identifies two to three stylistic elements and explains the contribution to effectiveness of the text.

Analyze how content contributes to effectiveness of text

ACT Connection	Objective
ARG 501	Students will be able to analyze how content contributes to effectiveness of text.

Measurable Task

Students compose a statement explaining the effectiveness of the text's purpose.

Students will be able to analyze the emphasis of details in multiple accounts of a single subject within different mediums. In higher level courses, students will evaluate multiple sources to answer a question or solve a problem.

Analyze various accounts for similarities and differences

ACT Connection

TST 501

Objective

Students will be able to analyze various accounts for similarities and differences.

Measurable Task

Students compose a paragraph that identifies significant similarities and differences, and explains the importance of the similarities and differences.

Determine which details are emphasized in various accounts on the same subject

ACT Connection

PPV 501

Objective

Students will be able to determine which details are emphasized in various accounts on the same subject.

Measurable Task

Provide students with a graphic organizer to locate and indicate similar details in various accounts and explain the emphasis on each of the accounts.

Analyze multiple sources of information from different media formats

ACT Connection

TST 505

Objective

Students will be able to analyze multiple sources of information from different media formats.

Measurable Task

Provide students with a graphic organizer where students locate and indicate similar details in different media formats and explain the emphasis on each of the accounts.

Evaluate multiple sources of information from different media

ACT Connection	Objective
SYN 501	Students will be able to evaluate multiple sources of information from different media.

Measurable Task

Students compose paragraph that analyzes information from at least two sources of different media for effectiveness.

Analyze multiple sources to answer a question

ACT Connection	Objective
SYN 501	Students will be able to analyze multiple sources to answer a question.

Measurable Task

Students compose a paragraph that analyzes information from at least two sources to answer a specific question.

Analyze multiple sources to solve a problem

ACT Connection	Objective
SYN 501	Students will be able to analyze multiple sources to solve a problem.

Measurable Task

Students compose a paragraph that analyze information from at least two sources to solve a problem.

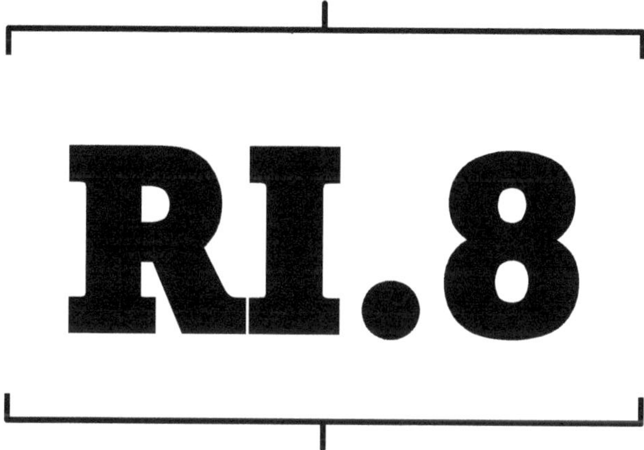

Students will be able determine if an argument or specific claim is valid. Students will be able to determine if evidence is valid and is effective at supporting the claim, which also means identifying false or fallacious reasoning. In higher level courses, students will evaluate legal reasoning in seminal U.S. documents.

Determine the validity of an argument

ACT Connection	Objective
TST 505	Students will be able to determine if an argument is valid.

Measurable Task

Students compose a statement asserting or refuting the validity of the argument and providing reasons for their assessment.

Determine false statements

ACT Connection	Objective
CLR 502	Students will be able to determine false statements.

Measurable Task

Provide students with a excerpt of a text to identify statements that are false.

Determine if reasoning for a argument is valid

ACT Connection	Objective
CLR 504	Students will be able to determine if reasoning for a argument is valid.

Measurable Task

Students compose a statement asserting or refuting the validity of the two pieces of evidence and providing reasons for their assessment.

Analyze an argument's validity

ACT Connection	Objective
TST 505	Students will be able to analyze an argument's validity

Measurable Task

Students compose a paragraph that analyzes an argument's validity by explaining how pieces of evidence from the text support the argument.

Evaluate argument and claims in a text

ACT Connection	Objective
TST 503	Students will be able to evaluate argument and claims in text.

Measurable Task

Students compose a paragraph that evaluates an argument's claims and explains the effectiveness of the claims.

Evaluate if evidence is relevant and sufficient

ACT Connection	Objective
ARG 501	Students will be able to evaluate if evidence is relevant and sufficient.

Measurable Task

Students compose a paragraph that evaluates an argument's evidence for relevance and explains the effectiveness of the claims.

Evaluate validity of reasoning in a argument

ACT Connection	Objective
ARG 501	Students will be able to evaluate validity of reasoning in an argument.

Measurable Task

Students compose a paragraph that evaluates an argument's evidence for validity and explains the effectiveness of the evidence.

Determine author's purpose in pivotal US and world texts

ACT Connection	Objective
PPV 502	Students will be able to determine author's purpose in pivotal US and world texts.

Measurable Task

Students compose a statement that determines the author's purpose in a pivotal U.S. document and world text.

Determine rhetorical reasoning in pivotal US or world texts

ACT Connection	Objective
WME 504	Students will be able to determine rhetorical reasoning in pivotal US or world texts.

Measurable Task

Students composea statement that determines rhetorical reasoning in a pivotal U.S. document and world text.

Analyze rhetorical reasoning in pivotal US or world texts

ACT Connection	Objective
WME 502	Students will be able to determine rhetorical reasoning in pivotal US or world texts.

Measurable Task

Students compose a paragraph that analyzes rhetorical reasoning in a pivotal U.S. document and world text by explaining how pieces of rhetorical evidence from the text supports the argument.

Students will be able to analyze the historical significance of U.S. documents. In higher level courses, students will be able to analyze period-specific documents for historical significance based on their theme, purpose, and rhetorical features.

Determine historical significance of a U.S. seminal document

ACT Connection	Objective
REL 505	Students will be able to determine historical significance of a U.S. seminal document.

Measurable Task

Have students compose a statement determining the historical significance of a U.S. seminal document.

Analyze the historical significance of a U.S. seminal document

ACT Connection	Objective
REL 502	Students will be able to analyze the historical significance of a U.S. seminal document.

Measurable Task

Have students create a paragraph analyzing the historical significance of a U.S. seminal document by explaining the impact specific statements have on the country and groups within the country.

Determine the purpose of a period-specific document

ACT Connection	Objective
REL 505	Students will be able to determine the purpose of a period-specific document.

Measurable Task

Have students compose a statement determining the purpose of the document used/created within a specific time period.

Analyze the purpose of a period-specific document

ACT Connection	Objective
REL 502	Students will be able to analyze the purpose of a period-specific document.

Measurable Task

Have students compose a paragraph analyzes purpose of the document used/created within a specific time period and explains the claims effect on the time period.

Determine the significance of a time period specific document

ACT Connection	Objective
REL 505	Students will be able to determine the significance of a time period specific document.

Measurable Task

Have students compose a statement determining the significance of a document from a specific time period.

Analyze the significance of a time period specific document

ACT Connection	Objective
REL 502	Students will be able to analyze the significance of a time period specific document.

Measurable Task

Have students compose a paragraph that analyzes the significance of the document in a specific time period and explains the impact on the time period.

Acknowledgments

This book was made possible by many people. Each individual played a crucial role in my realization of need, my motivation to complete, and the time spent to edit.

Staci, without your encouragement this would not have been possible. Thank you for going through the first draft and asking me to explain every step so that I could see every task through someone else's eyes.

Tara, thank you for helping me believe in myself enough to get this done. Your guidance on what needed to be included and when my ideas were just a little too fucking big was crucial to completing the task. Thank you for putting up with my late nights and for killing your eyes as you checked for every comma, repetitive word, and shit that didn't make sense.

Annmari and Nikki, your constant cheerleading kept me moving throughout this project. When I thought I would succumb to complete brain death from analyzing every standard, you each were present to remind me that I can get this shit done and help a lot of teachers.

Leigh, Jessica, Ali, Kennedy, and Sam: each of you opened my eyes to the vast need for a resource like this. The time you spent working with me and helping me hone my skills was critical to my completion of this project. My only hope is that this makes your job easier.

www.ingramcontent.com/pod-product-compliance
Ingram Content Group UK Ltd.
Pitfield, Milton Keynes, MK11 3LW, UK
UKHW021919190726
13853UKWH00002B/750

9 798492 120634